How to surviv
from nine to f

*Other books by Jilly Cooper
published by Methuen*

How to Stay Married
Jolly Super
Jolly Super Too
Jolly Superlative
Superjilly
Supercooper
Jolly Marsupial
Class
Intelligent and Loyal
Super Men and Super Women
The Common Years
How to Survive Christmas
Turn Right at the Spotted Dog

Jilly Cooper

How to survive from nine to five

drawings by
TIMOTHY JAQUES

A Methuen Paperback

A Methuen Paperback

First published in Great Britain 1970
by Methuen & Co. Ltd
Published in one volume with *How to Stay Married*
as *Work and Wedlock* 1977 by Methuen Paperbacks Ltd
This edition published 1988
by Methuen London
Michelin House, 81 Fulham Road, London sw3 6rb
Copyright © 1970, 1977 by Jilly Cooper
Drawings © 1970 by Methuen & Co. Ltd

Printed and bound in Great Britain
by Richard Clay Ltd, Bungay, Suffolk

British Library Cataloguing in Publication Data

Cooper, Jilly, *1937–*
   How to survive from nine to five.
   I. Title
828′.91407

   ISBN 0-413-19460-4

To Derek and Christine

Contents

How to survive from nine to five

introduction

From the conservative dark
Into the ethical life
The dense commuters come
Repeating their morning vow
I *will* be true to the wife,
I'll concentrate more on my work.

W. H. Auden.

It is nearly nine years since I had a proper nine to five job, but as I sit here typing in the garden looking at a torrent of bright pink roses, and watching my son dig up plants and sprinkle earth over the cats, I am still haunted by the days I spent working in an office.

Offices, you see, are for organization men, and I— being a dyed-in-the-wool disorganization woman —was a disaster as an employee, getting through more than twenty jobs in thirteen years.

My first job, which was the only one I really loved, was as a cub reporter on a local paper. The editor was a wild Irishman who wrote like a dream when he wasn't drinking like a fish. At the end of six months, he amazed the inhabitants of the town by walking the length of the High Street with a pink plastic chamber-pot on his head. A week later I came in on Monday morning to find him crouched on top of his desk, squawking morosely, an empty whiskey bottle beside him.

"I'm a seagull," he said after a few minutes, "and I shall fly around and do it on anybody I don't like."

At lunchtime, the Office Crone noticed him and immediately telephoned the newspaper proprietor at head office. Later in the day, a plain van came to take him away.

I'm a seagull

It was the first instance of many in office life when the right but repulsive prevailed over the wrong but romantic. After that a more sober editor was appointed, but the job never again reached the same peaks of inspired lunacy, and a few months later, lured by Mayfair and the fleshpots, I left journalism to become an account executive in a public relations firm.

After that the jobs came fast and furious – copywriter, editor, publisher's reader, receptionist for a motor firm, demonstrator at Earl's Court, temporary typist, a nymphomation officer in advertising, a telephonist, a puppy-fat model, and finally even a director of a company. So I can say truthfully that I have a non-working knowledge of most levels of the office caste system.

Offices, I found, were too much like school. There was the same nightmarish first day, when it was better to be seen and not heard, the same hierarchy, where it was not done to make close friends with one's seniors or one's juniors, the Personnel Department in a permanent state of bossy bustle like Matron and her minions, the notice boards on which pointless messages were pinned, lunches in the canteen exactly like school dinners, the responsible members of the staff behaving like form prefects, board meetings like staff meetings ('what are they saying, are they discussing me?') and finally, whether you're a writer or a typist, the awful sense of handing in your prep and having it returned the next day: 'C+. Could do better.'

The only difference is that as schools get paid (instead of paying you for your services) they are less trigger happy about booting you out than offices are.

I was the one that got away, but I still think of the thousands of people fighting their way to the office every morning.

Getting a job

Having had so many jobs in my life, I consider myself an expert at interviews. Never be depressed by the high-powered-sounding advertisements on the Appointments pages, the columns and columns of ads offering *unique* opportunities at attractive salaries to the right candidate: "We are looking for a young dynamic engineer," they say, "someone with drive and enthusiasm and a keen interest in re-inforced concrete, who is willing to settle in Australia. A knowledge of explosives would be useful."

The Advertising ones are even worse: "We at Fishbone, Codpiece and Nutter aren't afraid of competition. We're looking for a young creative genius who can write us all into the ground."

Hey there, Girl Friday

The sits. vac. for persons aren't much better: "Hey there, Eunuch Friday. I'm looking for someone to step into my shoes (size nine) and look after the most lovable Production Manager in the world. I wouldn't be deserting him if I weren't expecting a baby next month. Luncheon Vouchers, sickness

benefit" (morning presumably) "three weeks holiday."
They're always wanting: "Very fast shorthand typists"
when you have given up sex for Lent, or offering
"Mature persons periods of exposure at Board Level",
whatever that may mean.

Even when you've found the kind of job you're looking
for, there are phrases to watch: "The successful
candidate will be expected to deputise for the departmental head in his absence," which means the
departmental head is probably an alcoholic or a sex
maniac.

"We're looking for a person who can introduce staff
changes where necessary." They're chicken about
doing their own sacking.

"Capable, unflappable person, who is not afraid of
hard work needed for busy office." They're a lot of
layabouts, and you'll be flat out from 9 a.m. to 9 p.m.

The letter of application is the next hurdle. It should
be a masterpiece of fiction, papering over all the cracks.
Get it properly typed on decent writing paper. Never
let it run over the page, people get bored with reading.
Never send a roneoed curriculum vitae, or start off:
"Dear Sir, You need me/I'm the man you are looking
for," which automatically puts people off.

If you've changed jobs many times, pick out the five
most impressive ones, and pretend they lasted longer
than they did. Always conceal long patches when you
were out of work. Never say you left a job for "personal
reasons". No one will believe you.

Before you're given an interview you may well be sent
one of those terrible questionnaires to fill in about
what games you excelled in at school, and whether the
parrot's had any serious illness and what sex you are.
Pure 1984. Resist the temptation to mob them up. Be
careful, too, of those eleven plus psychology tests:
"Which is the odd man out—goat, ardvaak, warthog,
giraffe, snuffbox, goose, Tramps?" It's sure not to be

Tramps.

If they ask you to pick out the doodle you like best avoid the one with lots of squiggles, which means you're over-sexed, and avoid circles outside the triangle, which is supposed to prove that you're too homeloving and will rush out of the office at four thirty every afternoon.

WHAT TO WEAR AT THE INTERVIEW
MEN

The most expensive cigars

For the budding executive you still can't go wrong with tapered charcoal and the old school tie. But at present, there is a swing away from the pink-and-white-faced Etonian with his rolled umbrella, so you may do better to wear a corduroy suit, no tie and flatten your 'a's when you talk. Exude an air of affluence, rich but not gaudy, silk shirt, gold cuff links, aftershave. Never smoke, especially if you've got bitten nails, but if you must, let it be the most expensive cigars (never from the packet or the tin). This is particularly imposing in a woman.

If you're applying for any kind of creative post, however – designer, copywriter etc. – the wilder you look the better: beards, jerseys inside your shirt, medallions, everything hanging round your neck except women. Get a calligrapher to write your letter of application for you, and remember to say nothing at the interview—as they expect young genius to be totally inarticulate.

Be careful about too long or too short hair. Equal pay for women is the law now—but the prejudices remain.

GIRLS

I suppose I never dressed so well in any office where I worked as on the first time I crossed the threshold. I became such an expert at bulling myself up for the interview, they never recognised me when I turned up in my normal scruff order on the first day of work.

Always tie your hair back. I once learnt that I was turned down for one job purely because mine fell over my eyes. The choice of scent is tricky. Plump optimistically for *Je Reviens* if you are seeing a man, *4711* if it's a woman. And it's a good idea to carry a spotless pair of gloves in a paper bag, to be whisked out just before you go into the interview.

Make-up is a more difficult problem. Will the bedroom eyes conceal the bedpost legs? And if you tart up too much there are always those direct males who are far more interested in offering you extra-mural activities: "I haven't anything for you right now, Miss Nitwit-Thompson, but let me take down your particulars. 722-4910 did you say? Splendid, splendid."

I haven't anything for you, Miss Nitwit-Thompson

THE INTERVIEW PROPER

Go to lots of interviews, at least one a month even when you don't need a job, to keep in training for when you do.

There are several important points to bear in mind.

1. Never reveal you're out of work even if your wife, children and parrot are starving. Jobs are like sex, the harder you play to get, the more they want you. Give the impression you can take or leave their lousy job.

2. Look cheerful. A chum of mine who deserves a degree in amiability went after a very high-powered advertising job. The interview had only lasted two minutes when the telephone went, it was the interviewer's mistress on the line and he discussed a forthcoming jaunt to Paris with her for the next twenty-five minutes, by which time the next candidate was due. My chum had just sat there looking amiable and unembarrassed. To his amazement he got the job, and later when he looked up details of his interview in the Confidential File, it said: "Keen,

co-operative, a good mixer, asked deeply searching questions about the nature of our business."

Boast about your capabilities

3. Remember to boast about your capabilities. Any idiot can sit on a board or take a job at chief executive level. But be careful of claiming specialised knowledge like space selling, or you may find yourself orbiting the earth and not able to get down.

4. If you're interviewed by the managing director, Mr Compton Ricket, and on the wall hangs a portrait of the late Sir Angus Compton Ricket, and suddenly

young Mr Compton Ricket, just down from Oxford, pops in so Daddy can OK his expenses, don't touch the job. You'll find there are seven deadly sons between you and that seat on the Board.

5. Phrases like "Only £15,000, the fringe benefits had better be good", never go amiss.

6. Too many people, when they go for interviews, are more interested in giving a good impression than finding out what the job is about. Remember it's you who ask the questions:

You: Why did the previous chap leave?

Interviewer: Of his own accord.

You: Not satisfied with working for you, eh?

7. Always put the interviewer at his ease. As soon as you enter the room, tell him to sit down and smoke if he likes.

8. An excellent precaution is to ask the interviewer to give you references from three previous employees.

9. Never sign a contract before you've sorted out paid holidays, free houses, free cars, bonus, pension, etc. You won't be in a position to bargain once they've got you in their clutches.

10. Finally, there's the question of references. You must have some mates willing to perjure themselves and add a few handles to their names.

Your euphoria at landing a plum job will soon give way to dismay, then panic, as your month's notice comes to an end. Will anyone speak to you; have you oversold yourself; will you be able to hold down the job?

You will suddenly become very loth to leave your old colleagues, particularly when they give you a riotous send off and club together to buy you a gilt tray or one piece of everything belonging to a dinner service you've always wanted. Don't forget to thank them. The letter will be pinned on the notice board and should begin:

'Dear All,
Denise and I were delighted with the tea tray you so kindly gave me. We have put it on the mantelpiece in the lounge, and it will serve as a constant and happy reminder of all the good times I had at No. 48.'

The newcomer

THE FIRST DAY

The first day at any office is absolute hell. When I'm king I shall make it law that everyone starts a new job on Friday instead of Monday. Monday morning, in particular, couldn't be a worse time. All the incumbents are feeling anti-establishment, ill tempered and are desperately trying to catch up on all those very urgent things that didn't seem to matter a damn on Friday.

Monday morning is also No Man's Land, a limbo between home and the office. The staff have been isolated from each other for two days over the weekend, and have lost any corporate enthusiasm, which will only emerge about Thursday. By Friday it will be joined by excitement about the coming weekend and they will feel in a good enough mood to give newcomers the welcome they deserve.

As it is, you arrive about 8.30 sick with nerves to find the building locked or deserted except for the odd cleaner morosely pushing a squeegee over the floor. You then kick your heels in Reception until a few 'sekketries' (as they describe themselves) arrive from the country lugging pigskin suitcases and the pick of Daddy's herbaceous border (which will either be arranged in jam jars, or block the basins of the Ladies for the rest of the week).

About eleven o'clock, Miss Hitler from Personnel will bustle up and cause a rumpus because you've forgotten your P.45 and your insurance cards. She will then direct you to your office. If you are an executive you will either find an in-tray groaning with bucks other people have passed, or even worse, a completely bare desk with empty drawers and an empty filing cabinet, and you'll sit gazing at a huge sheet of virgin blotting paper, wondering what to write with all those sharpened pencils.

It's also possible that there's no job and you've just been brought in to swell the shadow Managing Director's faction in office politics. The sekketry promised you has decided to work for someone else (a blessing because you've no work for her anyway) and the rest of the department are wearing black ties and flying the Office Crone at half mast in mourning for your predecessor, whom they consider was unfairly ousted.

Occasionally people will shuffle into your office and say: "Oh, you're the new chap," and shuffle out again. Endeavour to appear busy. One man I know brought in at a very senior level wrote a novel during his first three months. Thinking he was writing reports, everyone was deeply impressed. Ask for progress reports for the last year (this will throw them, because they probably don't have any), or files, or the minutes of recent meetings. Then you can fill in your time, shuffling papers back and forth, frowning and nodding gravely. Soft pedal the hatchet approach: "I'm a new chap, just getting my sea legs, perhaps you can help me," will work wonders.

If you join as a sekketry you will probably be fobbed off with a desk with uneven legs, and an old battleship of a typewriter which everyone else has rejected and which tabulates automatically every time you press the A key.

An old battleship of a typewriter

Suddenly a choleric, fire-breathing old man will rush out of a nearby office, shout at you and rush back again. Alas, that is the cosy pink-faced sherry-bestowing old gentleman who seemed such a darling when he interviewed you last month. Bosses are invariably April when they woo, December when they wed. He wants you to take dictation.

Nearby sekketries will not speak to you except to tell you what a snake he is, and that everyone's leaving the firm because he's so vile to work for. You daren't interrupt their Monday morning panic with questions, so you will automatically have to re-type all your letters tomorrow because you didn't know about the lilac flimsy for the Art Department, or not putting a full stop after the date.

Remember to bring in two large shopping baskets to smuggle out all the botched-up letters you have to throw away. Miss Hitler from Personnel will not be amused by those brimming waste-paper baskets of scrumpled paper.

You will sit crossing your legs wondering how much longer you can hold out because no one has told you the firm shares a loo with Golberg's Imported Goatskins on the next floor.

At twelve-fifteen someone looks at her watch and says with obvious relief, "I should go to lunch now", then they can all discuss you.

Not knowing where to go, you will be deceived by the peeling paint and gloomy exterior of a little place on the corner which will turn out to be French and cost you at least a fiver.

Then there's the ghastly prospect when you get back to the office dead on 1.15 of how you're going to survive until 5. Although the work is piling up, you're terrified to type because you do it so slowly compared with the rest of the sekketries, whose hands are moving over the keys with the speed and dexterity of concert pianists. By tea time you're so grateful to some whiskery old boot for offering you a Lincoln cream that you strike up a friendship you'll never be able to shake off.

There are, however, advantages in being a newcomer. Everyone expects you to be inoperative for the first six months anyway, and you can blame every mistake you make on your predecessor.

On my father's first day at Fords, he was sent down to the foundry to report to the chief metallurgist. When he arrived one man seemed to be giving all the orders, so he turned to a nearby workman and asked if this man was the metallurgist.

"No Buddy," came the reply, "I think he's a Russian."

The hierarchy

Give people enough rope, and they'll hang you.

If you are to survive from nine to five, you must understand that nothing is more rigid than the office caste system, which is based on the premise that subordinates, unless kept ruthlessly in their place, will cheek you when you try to pull rank on them.

It is therefore unwise to risk being seen more than once in the company of a high-ranking member of the firm; people will suspect sexual commitment or political intrigue.

Nor is it done for women executives to go to lunch with the sekketries unless it's a birthday treat. Also, remember that if one of your old mates is promoted over you, your relationship will never be the same again. In no time he'll be goose-stepping all over you – power élite swagger and all.

Members of the staff, however, are always trying to wriggle their way up the hierarchy, typists calling themselves sekketries, sekketries calling themselves personal assistants, senior sekketries signing themselves Sekketry to the Deputy Managing Director whenever the Managing Director goes on holiday.

There will also be ridiculous wrangling over whether you are high enough up the ladder to rate a teaspoon or a bone china tea set with roses on it. In some firms they even have a special directors' lavatory, the only difference being that they have two kinds of loo paper – hard and very hard. If a woman were promoted to the board, it would be interesting to see if she would be expected to use it.

Your actual hierarchy will most probably consist of:
The Office Junior who knows nothing and does everything.
The Sekketry who knows everything and does nothing.

The Office Deb who knows everybody, my dear, and does nothing.

The pink and white Etonian trainee who knows the Office Deb.

The Personal Assistant who knows nothing and does nothing.

The Executive who interferes and prevents everyone from doing anything.

The Deputy Head of Department who panics.

The Head of the Department who signs letters, writes his report and doesn't give a damn because he's retiring at the end of the year.

The Managing Director, who can't read anyway.

Let us now look more closely at a few members of the hierarchy.

THE BOSS

Work hard and you will be rewarded by the promotion of your superiors.

Some bosses are good, some are not. Try very hard to give yours some responsibility. Bosses with nothing to do will always poke their noses into your affairs.

Here are some typical bosses:

THE BULLY

He can't leave his staff alone and bullies them into a state of jibbering inefficiency because it makes him feel superior. Stress is transmitted down the hierarchy until even the messenger boys are on tranquilizers. Like the circumlocution office, the bully is always beforehand in the art of seeing how not to do things. Stand up to him, or leave immediately before mental paralysis sets in.

THE MAN ON THE MAKE

He certainly won't want to make you, you're not important enough. He'll be far too busy sucking up to senior sekketries and the Managing Director's wife.

He will take credit if anything goes right, but you will carry the can if anything goes wrong.

A favourite expression will be: "I'm going to give you a free hand with this one," (but he'll keep a free foot to boot you out if you make a hash of it.) Or "You're going to have rather fun with this," before he hands you 20 pages of figures to type.

THE DREAMING BOFFIN

You'll spend your time sewing on buttons, collecting brief cases from the lost property office and rushing in with the fire extinguisher when he sets his waste-paper basket on fire. When he dictates he will probably eat his biscuits, then your biscuit, then drink his tea, then your tea. He will carry his washing round in his brief case, and suddenly pull out his underpants by mistake and say: "Would you possibly mind typing this for me?"

THE ARISTOCRAT

Work for him and you've got a cushy number. He will wear tweeds on Thursday for going to the country and he will not return until Tuesday morning. He will also be inoperative during the summer months, going to Ascot and Henley etc. Your time will be spent answering invitations, ordering caviar from Fortnums, and finding out how to address Duchesses and Earls on envelopes.

Moving down the hierarchy we come to:

THE EXECUTIVE

Avoid thought, it inevitably clouds the issue.

The executive has nothing to do except decide what is to be done, tell someone to do it, listen to reasons why they shouldn't do it, or why it should be done differently, and think up a crushing and conclusive reply. A week later he will follow up to see the thing has been done, discover it has not been done, ask why it hasn't been done, and listen to excuses from the person who didn't do it.

He will then wait another week before making further investigations, and avoid the temptation to wonder why he didn't do it himself in the first place. It would have taken him five minutes, instead it has taken a fortnight to find out that someone has taken at least a week to do it wrong. He then sits back and decides it's good for subordinates to learn by their own mistakes.

DEADWOOD

Nothing venture, nothing lose.

A step further down the hierarchy you will find the men the bosses hang their coats on – poor old dodderers in their late fifties, their false teeth rattling with nerves. Loss of pension hangs over their heads like a sword of Damocles. Knowing that they won't get another job if they're fired, they refuse to stick their necks out.

Weighed down by megaworries, the Dodderer will be convinced that people who couldn't even plot their way to the loo are conspiring against him. Shut doors will drive him into a frenzy, and every time he hears a typist whispering, even if it's only asking her next door neighbour if she can borrow a tampax, he's convinced she's whispering about him.

Home-made fishpaste sandwiches

At lunchtime, he takes a packet of home-made fishpaste sandwiches out of a shabby brief case. Occasionally at weekends, he gets drunk on Guinness. He often develops crushes on ugly typists.

Beneath this trembling exterior, however, lies a knight of the festering grievance, who can generate quite a force of discontent around the office.

Avoid antagonising him. He sneaks like wildfire.

PIGGIES

Piggies exist in most firms. They are sly, insensitive, unimaginative and always eating, particularly toffees, which they suck noisily and never offer to anyone else. Piggies never rise to the top of the tree, but they never get ulcers. They irritate subordinates and superiors equally, but are never fired because they are moderately efficient. Never work for a Piggy. Once you are directly below one in the hierarchy you will never rise to the top of the tree either.

THE PERSONNEL DEPARTMENT

Usually manned by a mini-bitch, who goes round measuring skirt lengths and calling sekketries by their surnames. Often she'll crouch for hours in the loo waiting to catch staff in indiscreet gossip.

Personnel are supposed to help you to hire people, but most of their day is spent forcing the squarest pegs into round holes. Whenever a new sekketry is required, they produce two identically grey, ugly, characterless girls to choose from.

Personnel departments are always having pointless economy drives. Even executives have to waste a ridiculous amount of time cajoling another biro out of them. In one office I remember the Personnel director hanging two rolls of lavatory paper, Bronco and Andrex, out of a top storey window to see which was the longer.

In another, the four members of the Personnel

department decided to go to Ireland together for the weekend on a special outing but insisted on flying on separate planes like the Royal Family, as the loss to the firm would have been so immeasurable if they had all been killed off in one go.

The Office Crone

THE OFFICE CRONE

She usually runs the typing pool. As soon as she arrives she puts on her mauve office cardigan to stop her 'good' clothes getting dirty. All her energies are channelled into bullying the typing pool like galley-slaves, and satisfying her insatiable appetite for new office equipment: dictaphones, electric typewriters, roller towels and Imperial Leather in the Ladies.

Much of her day will be spent foraging inside her transparent cream-coloured blouse to haul up a bra strap, eating biscuits, and surreptitiously plucking out her beard with a bulldog clip. She will be driven to frenzy by two things: lateness even if it's only thirty seconds, and mislaying her fingerette, which is a rubber thimble covered in spikes which looks like some weird Indian erotic device, but is actually used for turning pages quickly.

Sucking up is the only way to woo her. Hold her wool for her, ask her advice on beauty problems, give her the odd bar of Turkish Delight as a present.

One of her arch enemies will be:

Miss Nitwit-Thompson

THE OFFICE DEB

Miss Nitwit-Thompson, a decorative quarter-wit who comes wrapped in cashmere and scotch mist on the end of a long yellow Labrador. She is working for a pittance "because the job sounded so interesting," and is always having time off to go to mid-week weddings. She takes long weekends, and invariably rings Mummy on Friday and asks her to "stop the train".

Originally employed for her style and "lovely speaking voice" which would impress clients and Americans on the telephone. She is usually hogging the telephone making personal calls to Jeremy, Caroline or Fiona to discuss last night's ball.

Another of the Office Crone's sworn enemies is:

THE LITTLE HOME-BREAKER

The office sex kitten, who has a lived-in look about her and is far more preoccupied with outgoing males than outgoing mail. The only filing she does is to file her nails, and the only use she makes of the office pencil sharpener is to sharpen her eye-pencil and her claws. She is not to be dismissed, however, for she usually knows a lot of high-level secrets, leaked by chief executives in moments of passion. She is also quite capable of hooking the Managing Director, and suddenly becoming the Boss's wife.

THE LITTLE HOME-MAKER

Who puts sticky buds in jam jars on her boss's desk, and is always whisking round with a feather duster and percolating coffee. She will spend more time indulging her "office beautiful" pretensions than actually typing. When asked what she does at parties she will call herself a Personal Assistant.

THE UNDIPLOMATIC BAG

The senior sekketry who will guard her boss with such ferocity that she's quite likely to keep important clients and the Managing Director away from him until everyone forgets his existence. She will, however, be an excellent chucker-out if undesirables manage to insinuate themselves into his office.

Finally, we come to:

THE TYPING POOL

Generally called Maureen or Eileen. Their function in life seems to be to slop tea and type back letters that don't always make sense. If any of their carbons reach the files they will be spotted with rubbing-out smudges like a Dalmatian. Brainwashed by the system, they generally go to the loo in triplicate.

The Average Typist's Day, however, will go something like this:

9.10 Arrives generating bustle, hidden behind huge tinted spectacles, and muttering about de-railed carriages on the line. Disappears to the loo to tart up.

9.30 Removes typewriter cover, discusses what 'he' did and said last night, what television they saw, speculates on boss's mood, reads own and other typists' horoscopes in the morning papers.

10.00 Coffee break. Eats cheese roll.

10.15 Takes spare pair of shoes out of plastic bag in bottom drawer of desk. Changes into them.

10.30 Takes dictation.

10.45 Returns from dictation. Grumbles for thirty minutes about the horrible mood the boss is in.

11.15 Called to window by fellow typist to ogle comely man who is walking down the street. Snags tights on central heating, fills in hole with brown pencil.

11.40 Goes to loo to tart up.

12.00 Gone to dinner.

1.15 Returns with carrier bags, discusses dinner, eats Yoghurt and Mars Bar.

2.30 Boss comes back from lunch in better mood.

2.31 Goes to the loo to re-do face.

2.45 Tries to read shorthand back, holds book upside down.

3.00 Starts grumbling about non-arrival of tea.

3.15 Tea arrives, eats home-made cake out of paper bag, reads own and other typists' horoscopes in evening paper.

3.20 Types lethargically.

3.30 Slips out, ostensibly to the chemist's, so no one can ask why she's going.

4.00 Returns ostentatiously waving a Boots paper bag, which is actually full of make-up and tights.

4.10 Starts muttering about catching post, tidies ferociously for five minutes. Assembles one letter in large leather folder and gets it signed by boss.

4.30 Grabs floral plastic bag and joins queue for the loo for a good wash to get 'all the ink off my hands'.

4.45 Tears out of the office, muttering "must try and catch the early train tonight".

4.50 Building deserted.

THE OFFICE BOY

Office boys—the avant garde of the company—live in the postroom. In my day, they all used to smoke pot, strum guitars, and grow their hair halfway down their backs. Now they're all punk rockers. Invariably they get into trouble because the photographic machine decides to break down when they are photostating some writhing nude, or the roneo machine gives up the ghost when they are running off 500 copies of an obscene poem.

As an office boy you'll be paid a rotten salary, but you can make a bit on the side, taking buses whenever you have to deliver anything and charging up for a taxi.

The office boy's prime function is to give his superiors racing tips, keep them posted on what's top of the hit parade, and to rise eventually to Managing Director, so people can say: "I remember him when he was only an office boy."

When you get to the top, remember to sack all the

The office boy

people who knew you as an office boy. They won't take you seriously, and will instil lack of respect into their colleagues.

One office boy I know left a firm, made his packet and came back ten years later as a client. Not realising he had left, the Managing Director met him in the passage, handed him a parcel, and asked him to take it to the post office.

THE GRIPEVINE

"Our recording machine is broken—this is a person speaking."

Always chat up the switchboard girls, they wield

People who knew you as an office boy

enormous power. If you get across them they can
'forget' to take messages, keep you hanging about for
hours waiting for a line, cut you off, and, worst of all,
tip off Miss Hitler from Personnel that you've been
making too many private calls–one of the most
heinous of office crimes. They are also the hub of the
gripevine and extremely valuable as a source of gossip.
I also think that every member of the staff–particularly the men–should spend a day on the switchboard to see what pressures the telephonists are

subjected to. I arrived at a temporary job once, and was asked if I could man the switchboard. No switchboard was ever more rapidly unmanned: all those horrible flaps signifying incoming calls came down at the same time, and the discs indicating that someone wanted a line started flickering as well. Flap, flap, flicker, flicker, they went all morning, until I was reduced to a state of nervous collapse. "Just putting you through," I would say hopefully, cutting off the sales manager's deal-clinching call to Australia for the seventh time.

On the receiving end there are those terrible occasions when the switchboard closes down and your lover, who's been soaking in some drinking club all afternoon, suddenly decides to ring you up and gets straight through to the Managing Director, who has to walk down three flights of stairs to find you.

Or those awful personal calls that come through when a meeting is being held in your office, and you hold the telephone very close to your ear so no one else in the room can hear the flood of invective.

Every so often there is a purge on private calls which no one takes any notice of. In one office a circle of paper was stuck on every telephone saying: "Please be brief. No private calls allowed." Some iconoclast promptly whipped it off and stuck it on the door of the Gents.

Survival for the top brass

HINTS FOR BOSSES

Let us begin with a few tips for the Boss – particularly if he's the Managing Director.

The secret of success is to keep your staff at each others' throats then they won't gang up against you. Create a state of tension and frantic backbiting. Divide and Rule.

Secure allegiance from junior executives by promising them individually that someone must step into your shoes when you retire. When you go away—on holiday or on a business trip—ask each one to keep an eye on things for you.

Don't humiliate the pants off a member of your staff in front of one of his subordinates.

Make decisions and stick to them. Havering is the one thing that will make you unpopular.

Try and remember your staff's names and use them when you meet them in the passage. Then if you want to put any of them down, call them by somebody else's name.

Be available at least sometime during the day to listen to grievances even if you do nothing about them.

Don't say you want to wish all your staff a Merry Christmas at 5 o'clock on Christmas Eve, and then ring down at 5.15 and say you're too busy.

Bosses could also do with a bit of advice in the way they handle their sekketries.

Ask about her lover or cats

You will reap dividends if you take a polite interest in her life outside the office. Ask her about her lover or her cats occasionally.

Remember her birthday. It's quite easy to check the date with Personnel and put it in your diary.

When she comes back from lunch three hours late, scarlet in the face, lacquered down to the eyebrows, and looking like a cross between Medusa and Little Lord Fauntleroy, tell her her hair looks nice.

One of the most damaging things people can say about you is: "He can't keep a sekkretry." It's even worse than having V.D. Try not to turnover them too quickly.

HOW TO IMPRESS AS AN EXECUTIVE

Always give the impression you're working hard. It's like the story of the Messiah suddenly arriving at the Vatican. All the Vatican staff were thrown into a panic because they didn't know how to behave.

"It doesn't matter what you do," said the Pope. "Just look busy."

Or take a tip from the House of Lords throughout the war, who did nothing in particular but did it very well. Nothing gives a worse impression than an idle sekketry reading a book or painting her nails. Keep yours at full tilt, even if she's only typing her own personal letters with a pink and blue carbon underneath. If someone asks you if you're up to your ears, always say "yes". But if, on the other hand, your Managing Director wants you to do something worthwhile like Letrasetting a poster for his wife's baby show, agree to do it at once.

Suck up to the senior sekketries, admire their spangled hairnets, and drop Murray Mints into their pockets. This means they will sing your praises to their respective bosses, the directors, who probably don't gossip to anyone else. It will also ensure that you can get in to see the directors whenever you want to. Always chat up the directors' wives. The way to a man's heart is through his wife.

If you are over 26, get yourself married. Bachelors and queers are still, alas, regarded with suspicion. More often the former is assumed to be the latter.

Call your wife and children outlandish names like Brunhilda and Ethelred so the boss can remember them easily, and feel he's being good with you.

Whenever you get in early – get seen. Wander up and down the directors' floor with a piece of paper in your hand. Leave notes on people's desks: "8.45. Called in to see you; could you ring me back?" People never put the time on memos unless it's before or after hours.

Buy two identical overcoats which people identify as yours. Leave one hung up in your room when you leave the office early.

Only put in an appearance on Saturday morning when you know the Boss is going to be there.

Cultivate a good telephone manner:

"Bless you, bless you, lovely to talk to you, J.J., of course it's no trouble, we must meet and have lunch sometime, I'll ring you, bless you, love to Elizabeth, absolutely no trouble at all, bless you, bless you, well if you could pull the odd strings I'd be very grateful, all the best, J.J., goodbye." When you put down the receiver say, "Silly old bugger".

Get a night line plugged through to your office so that whenever a director wants one he's told you've already appropriated it and assumes you always work late.

Make yourself indispensable in some way. Be the only person who understands the crossest index system, or who has the energy to work out the table seating plan at the office dance.

Always be nice to everyone in the firm on the way up. You never know who you may meet on the way down. Most key managerial decisions are taken when the heads are down in the bunker. If the Managing Director is a golfer, take up golf, play it competently

but don't beat him too often.
Games and sex are the only really reliable ways to
bridge the hierarchy gap.

But don't beat him too often

Advice for the imperfect sekketry

Grumble first, think afterwards.
If your shorthand is slow, sit in front of your boss's
desk in your shortest skirt and, whenever he starts

dictating too fast, uncross and re-cross your legs very slowly. He'll stop in his tracks. Choose a boss whose office doesn't have Venetian blinds, then you can distract his attention by pointing out the Concorde or the first swallow when you need a moment to catch up. The tight sweater or the low-cut dress are the shoddy typist's allies. Hand him his letters, then stand with your hands behind your back or lean forward, and he won't notice any of the mistakes.

If you're going to be caught doing the crossword at least let it be *The Times*.

If you've got something terrible to confess, tell your boss in the afternoon when he comes back jolly from lunch, his mind scrambled with drink. Don't wait until five o'clock – when he will be suffering from a hangover.

Remember, in office life godliness comes a very poor second to cleanliness. Tidy hair, white blouses, skirts on the knee making no concession to Maxi or Mini, polished shoes are the things which gladden the heart of the Office Crone and Miss Hitler from Personnel. If you get across them – no matter how much your boss loves you – you'll soon be out on your ear.

Today most offices allow you to wear trousers. But they must pass the Nice Trouser Test – you won't get away with split jeans or Bermuda shorts. Keep a communal skirt in the cupboard which any sekketry can borrow if she's summoned to one of the more reactionary directors.

Keep your office tidy. Nothing irks the powers-that-aren't more than an untidy office. They suspect, quite rightly, that all sorts of documents are hidden beneath the rubble. One of the reasons I was such a disaster in the office was that I always built ramparts of paper round me, in the hope that people might forget about me altogether.

Don't, on the other hand, go to the opposite extreme. Most bosses regard an empty desk as an indication

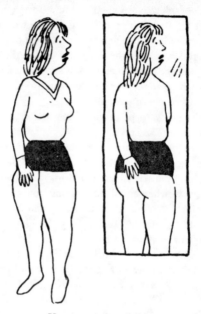

Keep a communal skirt

that you are under-employed. A few papers and files lying about will correct this impression.

Keep your out-tray from hitting the ceiling. One girl was sacked at one place I worked because, when told to do her boss's filing, she got languidly to her feet in front of the Personnel Dragon, picked up her boss's out-tray and calmly emptied it into the waste-paper basket.

Never, never throw any papers away – they're bound to be the one thing your boss asks you to turn up the very next day, so you spend fruitless hours scrabbling through dustbins full of empty tomato soup cans and cigarette butts.

THE PROTECTION RACKET

One of the sekketry's first duties is to cover up.

If the Managing Director wants your boss, even if he hasn't come in at all or left the building seven hours ago to "buy a packet of cigarettes," always say: "He's just popped out," or "He's in the building somewhere. I'll try and trace him."

After three o'clock never say he's not back from lunch, even if he isn't. It will give the impression he's lying on his back sozzled in El Vino's. Just say: "He popped in, and has just popped out again", or produce a tear-jerker excuse: "He's just slipped out to the shops to buy his wife/little daughter a birthday present."

THE TELEPHONE

Whatever your accent, as a sekketry you must put on a posh voice when you answer the telephone. If it's someone's sekketry wanting your boss, you will then have a tussle with her which may go on for hours over whose boss comes to the telephone first.

There are bound to be some people your boss will not want to talk to. If you're not sure say: "He's in a very important conference, I'll just see if he can be disturbed." Then find out if he will speak to them.

Or you can say: "He's tied up with the Managing Director's wife" (although it does give rise to terrifying bondage fantasies).

If you're stumped by a query, never betray ignorance, just say: "Ooo, my other telephone's ringing. I'll call you back later."

There are also ways of not revealing to your boss that you're making a personal call. Don't give a guilty start when he comes into the room and say nervously, "I must go now," and slam down the receiver.

Go on talking. Make remarks like: "That's extremely valuable, we must keep in close contact over this one. I'll find out some more details and figures and call you back later."

Then you can ring off and tell your boss it was a member of the public ringing up with some query, or a customer trying to flog you some office writing paper.

The office beautiful

Most people today are far too busy furnishing their offices to do any work. Half their day is spent firing off memos to the Personnel Department grumbling that the pile of their carpet is not deep enough and is a foot further away from the wall than the carpet of the man next door who has not been with the firm as long and is six months younger.

One of the reasons why bosses allow their staff to squander such vast amounts of the firm's money playing David Hicks is that if you make your office look like a "lovely home" they assume you're more likely to spend more time in it.

It's a mistake for the Managing Director to make his offices too lush. All the clients will think he's wasting their money, and all the staff will ask for rises.

But if he really wants to play the big tycoon he will paper his walls with grey flannel and cover the floor with a white shaggy rug. In one corner is a cocktail cabinet, in another a fridge for cooling down over-heated Office Crones. Six telephones sit on a huge black leather desk, along with the jade ashtrays, cigarette lighter and cigarette box filled with Russian cigarettes. No papers are in sight – it would be considered vulgar for anything like work to be carried on in such a rarefied atmosphere. Colleagues lounge on sofas round the room. Spotlights nestle in the walls casting pools of light on abstract paintings; after lunch they are dimmed so the maestro can cogitate or doze

Like a "lovely home"

or finger his very private secretary in a reflective manner.

The smaller fry must be careful not to be too extreme. One copywriter I know moved into a top level post in an advertising agency and was determined that his office should be unique – no black leather, or reproduction tat breathing beeswax. He spent a fortune of the firm's money on William Morris wallpaper, an antique desk and chairs, a Victorian grandfather clock, and finally a harpsichord on which he strummed in moments of inspiration.

The trade papers got very excited and photographed him *in situ*, until the rest of the staff got so jealous they staged a palace revolution and had him removed. Later he was sent a bill for the office.

Piggies live in offices like sties, the top drawer of their desks filled with toffee papers and cake crumbs. They are also sly enough to put a photograph of the Prime Minister or the Leader of the Opposition on their walls, depending on the political affiliations of the Managing Director.

Office happenings

There are certain occupations in offices which will not only get you through the day but also impress people.

THE MEMORANDUM

"The horror of that moment," the King went on, "I shall never, never forget!" "You will, though," the Queen said, "if you don't make a memorandum of it." Lewis Carroll.

Although it is the biggest time-waster in office life, you must never underrate the importance of the memo. You will be judged by the volume of your paper work. In offices today, the internal telephone is only used to conduct an affaire. If you ring a colleague up and tell him something important about work, he will wait patiently until you've finished, not listening to a word, and then say: "But you'll be sending me a memo about it anyway, won't you?"

The memo's chief function, however, is as a track-coverer, so that you can turn on someone six months later and snarl: "Well, you should have known about it, I sent you a memo."

It is also useful if you want to convince colleagues of your staggering burden of responsibility. Outlining your achievements in the last six months, you send a memo from yourself to yourself, but the latter is buried so deep in "cc." to other people that people are merely impressed and never realise to whom the memo is really being sent. The memo is also a status symbol. When people feel their position is really secure in a firm, they get their own memos printed: "From the pen (or the desk) of Caroline Nitwit-Thompson."

Such pomposity should not go unchallenged. Fire

48

back a memo: "From the occasional table of J. Cooper."
The memo of course is one of the strongest weapons
wielded by Miss Hitler from Personnel, who will fire
them off if someone is too prodigal with the guillotine,
or uses office elastic bands to hold her (or his) hair
back, or arrives a minute late in the morning.

Memos from the Managing Director should be read
before you make a paper dart out of them. Memos from
the legal department should also be taken seriously or
you may end up in gaol.

My favourite memo, however, was sent out by the
Media department of a big advertising agency: *"The
Muckshifter and Loader* has changed its name to *The
Muckshifter."*

MEETINGS

"The only meetings I like are between two people."
                                        Tennessee Williams.

Another king-sized timewaster. Twenty-four people
half asleep round a table making indecisions that only
concern a couple of those present anyway. Meetings,
however, are rather like cocktail parties. You don't
want to go, but you're cross not to be asked. They are
usually called by one person: the Sales Manager or
the Marketing Manager because–reluctant to act on
his own initiative–he wants official sanction for his
projects. Rising executives often call meetings to make
themselves feel important. A lot of meetings are held
to arrange when to have meetings.

Your certified rat will call meetings at 9.00 and 2.00 so
everyone arrives late, and it puts him one up.

Meetings today are usually called conferences to
make them sound more significant. Sales conferences
in particular are a nightmare. All that ghastly ra-rahing
and team rallying. A complete monologue from

49

The only meetings I like

the Managing Director punctuated by sycophantic laughter from the floor. It's rather like the end of term prize-giving, but unfortunately no one's going home for the holidays at the end of it.

Afterwards you have to attend a ghastly tea to meet the "reps", hideous heartiness prevails, bonhomie cubed, no one acts normally, everyone makes thumbs up signs to one another, and when you shake hands with someone you clasp his hand in both of yours.

In spite of all the rubbish talked about the miracle of the group think, new ideas very seldom emerge at meetings. If you've got a good idea, you're either too shy to produce it, or you keep it to yourself because you know it will be shot down or pinched by someone else.

A FEW TIPS

Save all your bad ideas for meetings. They'll be shot down, but you'll give the impression of being a bright young man.

If the meeting is going against you, steer the discussion round to cricket, which will hold up the proceedings for at least five minutes.

A good clash of wills stops everyone going to sleep. Argue ferociously against any ideas you secretly know are directly opposed to those of the Managing Director.

Combat sleep by deciding in order which people in the room you would most like to sleep with. Think what kind of animal they most resemble, and count the number of times a particular word like feasible, valuable, or meaningful is used.

If a rival of yours seems to be talking too persuasively and too long, distract everyone's attention by drawing a nude on your scribbling pad and reaching strategic parts of her anatomy as he is making his most telling points.

A rival talking too persuasively

One woman I knew used to smoke a pipe, and when she wanted to create a diversion she would get up,

wander down the table taking butts out of the ashtrays, tear them open and fill her pipe with the
tobacco.

Extra-mural activities

A lot of your working day will be spent out of the
office:

THE LUNCH HOUR
*Never drink black coffee at lunch; it will keep you awake
in the afternoon.*
Euphemistically called the lunch hour, this interval
in the day's inactivities runs from twelve to three-
thirty. This is the Piggies' High Noon when, snorting
with delight, they pour out of their offices like their
Gadarene forbears into the café opposite where they
eat three courses of soup, shepherd's pie and chips,
and treacle pudding followed by white coffee, after
which they waddle back to their office to eat biscuits
all afternoon.

The sekketries will reach peak activity during the
lunch hour, when they hare round doing their shopping, getting clothes out of the dry cleaners and
having their hair done. They also squeeze in three-
quarters of an hour to have lunch, sitting in each
other's laps in steamy coffee bars, fat girls eating
salads, thin girls eating spaghetti, their dissection of
last night's escapade only interrupted by the hiss of
the espresso machine.

Invariably just as they're getting down to a good bitch
about the office, they feel a heavy hand on their
shoulder; it will be Miss Hitler from Personnel asking
if she can join them.

Office Crones seldom go to lunch, but spend their hour
brewing tomato soup in the basement (or, because

A heavy hand on their shoulder

they're on a diet, sourly nibbling at cottage cheese and
a piece of celery), adding another two rows to their
green open-work jersey, and waiting to tear latecomers
limb from limb.

Then, of course, there's the office canteen, with its
menu improperly typed by one of the sekketries.

> Clean Soup
> Boiled button
> Stewed rears and naked egg custard.

Unless you want fat meat or the boniest piece of the
fish, it's essential to waste a great deal of time chatting
up the woman who runs the canteen. (She's the only
woman in whom the Piggies display any interest.)

Meanwhile the directors are roughing it at the Ritz.

If you are to get on as an executive, you must realise that in order to do business with anyone, you must down two large pink gins, a three-course lunch with a good bottle of claret, and two double brandies, not forgetting cigars, at every stage of the deal.

How well I remember those nightmarish business lunches when I was a very junior Public Relations executive, entertaining lady journalists and wondering desperately what would be the right moment to tell them about the product I was supposed to be trying to flog.

Usually I funked it until the coffee stage, then said timidly, "Well-er about these fascinating rubber gloves." And the lady journalist would glance at her watch, mutter about a deadline, leap to her feet, thanking me profusely for a divine lunch, and disappear double quick out of the restaurant...

It always seems a slight anomaly that managements expect their executives to spend at least a tenner a day on lunch, then only issue the rest of the staff with 15p luncheon vouchers. I suppose this ensures wakefulness in the afternoon. No one could sleep on a 15p lunch.

A friendly grocer will usually exchange your vouchers for groceries. I used to buy cigarettes with mine.

LUNGE HOUR

The lunch hour is invariably followed by the lunge hour. This is the period of rocketing libidos and octopus hands, when bosses and executives return from lunch swollen with insolence and wine, and make passes at their sekketries and any pretty girls who seem to be around.

SKIVING

Thou shalt not kill time—shirkers of the world, unite.

It never hurts of course to put in an occasional

appearance in the office if only to make a few private calls, put your personal letters through the franking machine, and collect your expenses before going to lunch.

When I worked in an office, I was past-mistress at the art of skiving. I always used to arrange to see someone at 10.30 (which meant I needn't go into the office beforehand) and to deliver something by taxi at five o'clock (which meant I could take the taxi on home afterwards and charge it up on expenses).

One ploy – if you're very late in the morning – is to take off your coat and hide it, with your shopping bag, in a chum's office, then wander into your own, giving your boss the impression you've been in for hours discussing affairs of state on the directors' floor.

When you get back very late from lunch, distract people by bringing back a Fuller's cake to be shared round, or a pair of gardening gloves for the Office Crone.

Getting out in the middle of the afternoon or the morning is more tricky. Try walking out or in with a large package under your arm, or pretend to be very religious. In one office where I worked, one of the copywriters was always wandering up to our woman boss and saying in an unctuous whisper: "It's a saint's day. I'm just nipping off to church, if you don't mind." She could then stay away anything up to four hours – it was only regarded as proof of her devotion. You can also say you're Jewish, which means lots of days off.

Creative people can perpetuate the myth that they work better at home because it's quieter, and then push off to the cinema. If you are "working at home", it's always a good idea to ring in from time to time and sound very businesslike.

Another excellent ruse is to ring up and say you're taking a day's holiday and won't be in. Personnel never check up. One colleague of mine took 40 days' holiday in a year as well as his official three weeks.

Or you can establish a reputation for being delicate—a dicky heart, a bad back—then if you don't come in people will assume it's playing up.

A reputation for being delicate

Never take more than three days off, or you'll be involved in dreary wrangles over doctor's certificates. It's also important to look very ill when you return bravely to work on the fourth day.

I perfected a "sickly looking" make-up which fooled everyone. Very pale foundation, green face powder to give you a livid look, brown mascara smudged under the eyes, and, most important of all, a touch of pink lipstick rubbed into the eyelids, accompanied by a stoical expression.

Ten to one you'll look so ill they'll send you home after lunch for another three days' holiday.

One company, conscious of the degree of absenteeism, sent round a memo to all staff headed *Loafing*, attacking the practice of slipping out for a couple of hours in the afternoon on the pretext of buying a loaf of bread.

HOLIDAYS

At the first pallid shaft of January sunlight, typists will plunge into cotton dresses, baring their grey arms and freckled bosoms to the world, and Miss Hitler from Personnel will issue the holiday list. Within ten days she will descend on you and give you a rocket for not making up your mind when you want to go.

Bosses are hell

Other heinous crimes (apart from not planning your holiday in January) include not looking forward to it with feverish enthusiasm, and not sending a postcard when you get there wishing quite untruthfully that the whole of the typing pool were with you.

As weeks pass, these postcards are sellotaped on the side of the filing cabinet, like swastikas on Spitfires, alongside the pin-up photographs of Robert Redford and James Hunt.

Bosses are hell after they come back from holiday or long business trips. They feel guilty about skiving and spending too much of the firm's money on trips to the game reserves or geisha girls, and assuage their guilt by having efficiency drives and finding fault with everything you've done right during their absence. The sekketry should pander to her boss's feelings, make a few minor but obvious mistakes for him to discover so he can feel that the wheels do not run completely smoothly without him. She should say she's pleased he's back, even if she's not. Everyone likes to feel missed.

Visitors

Occasionally in offices you will have visitors. The temporary secretary, for example.

THE TEMPORARY
"I spent a week in Production, a week in the Art Department, a week in Control, a week out of control."
Every office should invest in a temporary at least twice a year to act as office scapegoat, then she can be blamed for every misdemeanour uncovered in the next six months.

A letter, for example, that never reaches its destination?
The temporary must have written the wrong address.
Chewing gum parked beneath the boardroom table?
That must have been when the temporary took the
minutes. The failure of the roller towel in the Ladies?
Certainly the temporary's fault–she spent enough
time in there doing her face.

On one occasion when I did a stint of temporary typing
I worked for some engineers who kicked me out when
I got the giggles over a memo consigning: "four
hundred eccentric nipples to Rotterdam." I won't
elaborate on the week I spent at the Mechanical
Handling Exhibition, except to say the handling I
received was far from mechanical.

I also managed to last three weeks in an insurance
company because I pretended I had a title which
impressed them. The typing pool was run by a Crone
who bullied us all unmercifully. One day she went to
the dentist to get her fangs fixed, and the girl sitting
next to me asked me if I'd like to have a look at the
Crone's secret book.

It was hidden in her bottom drawer under packets of
squashed flies: a book of animal photographs, and
beneath each photograph she had pencilled in faintly
the name of a member of the firm. Beside a row of pigs
were four members of the Claims Department, beside
an evil-looking warthog, the Personnel Officer, beside
a sloth, the most idle member of the Pool.

"Oh look, she's added a new one," said my friend.

There, beside a picture of a white rat with terrified
eyes running round a treadmill, she had written:
Jilly Cooper.

The unkindest cut of all, however, was when the
agency sent me to a nursing organization staffed
almost entirely by women. In actual fact I and two
male nurses were the only "women" in the place.
Time and again I was pounced upon by Amazon after

Won't you become permanent, my dear?

Amazon in the canteen, under the desk, behind the filing cabinet. At last I heard those longed-for bass-baritone words: "Won't you become permanent, my dear?"

THE COMPUTER

"Our daily sales are now done by a commuter."

The computer was originally brought in as a high-salaried whizz kid, who made all the staff very edgy and worried about their jobs. Now they realise its limitations they are no longer worried. The computer lies exhausted in the basement, its digits set at ooooooooooooo. There has been a computer pogrom. No one knows what to do with it. It is not even allowed to pay salaries, as they're considered too confidential. It is inclined to pay people twice for work they haven't done. Its mistakes are sorted out by some undiplomatic bag in a grey dress.

It first disgraced itself because it sent 100 books to the West Indies instead of W.1. London.

All the departments that were abolished when the computer was installed are now creeping back under new names like Data Control and Central Control, and are staffed largely by temporaries.

Finally, an even more unwelcome but more frequent guest is the management consultant.

MANAGEMENT CONSULTANTS

Management consultants waste time, cost money, make the staff twitchy and are probably working for competitors. If by any chance your office is unfortunate enough to suffer a plague of them, there are certain tactics that can be employed. Always tell lies when they ask you questions about your work, by saying that everything takes you twice as long as it really does. Tell them the most horrifying stories about your superiors, but above all tell them how out-of-date and appallingly maintained every piece of office equipment is – and hint that the management are so at each other's throats that the only way of saving the firm is by removing practically every member of the board.

This not only gives you the faint hope of a better job yourself, but will be a distinct spur to the management consultant to create a plum job for himself. (Although they're not allowed to do this, we all know that they do.)

They will then introduce vast quantities of new office equipment (they're probably on a cut from the manufacturers) and will replace half the staff, but it will be necessary later to employ an entirely new set of people to maintain, manage and operate the equipment. These people will always command higher salaries than the ones the machinery replaced, thus the cost of them, plus the cost of the machinery, plus the management consultants' fee, coupled with the inevitable losses incurred by decreased efficiency all round, mean that the company is invariably far worse off than it was before.

I can only add an instance when the management consultants moved in on a symphony concert. Here are some of their findings:

"For considerable periods, the four oboe players had nothing to do. The number should be reduced and the work spread more evenly over the whole orchestra, thus eliminating peaks of activity."

"No useful purpose is served by repeating on the horns a passage that has already been played on the strings."

"All twelve of the violins played identical notes. The staff of this section should be drastically cut. It is estimated that if all the redundant passages were eliminated the whole concert time could be reduced to twenty minutes and there would be no need for an interval."

Office pastimes

BOREDOM

In any office you will have long passages of boredom. When I shared an office with a colleague we used to take it in turns to go through the telephone lists, pick out two people e.g. the Office Crone and Miss Hitler from Personnel, and say: "Which one would you rather go to bed with?" The other person had to make a snap decision before you counted five.

A great deal of the typists' time will be spent speculating about the lovelife of other members of the staff.

"She'd be quite attractive if she made more of herself," they agree, "but she ought to go on a diet" (which means she'll presumably make less of herself.

Miss Taylor in Accounts

Confusing?). Or they will discuss Miss Taylor in Accounts who's so very "refined and smart" they can't see why she isn't married.

On an executive level, the day will be passed discussing the respective merits of different hedge-clippers and insulation materials, talking about the greenhouse you are going to put up in the garden next week when you've finished wall-papering the dog's kennel, and telling your colleagues how you make home-made wine.

Grumbling is also a great time-waster. Listen politely to other people's moans, but never offer to help them out. We all know the moaner who spends all morning tearing his hair over his workload, and telling you he's heading for a crack-up. So you offer to do some of his work for him. He accepts with alacrity; the crack-up is halted in mid-stream. He will then go to lunch, and ring in about 3.30 to say he's a bit tied up and won't be back. Next morning he'll come staggering in and moaning once more about his workload.

SEX IN THE OFFICE

Dear Sir Stroke Madam

Offices vary: some are like monasteries, and the only thing you're likely to get raped by is the spacebar on the long-carriage typewriter. Others out-thrum *Peyton Place*. As an ex-colleague said: "You have to knock on people's office doors before you go in, not out of courtesy, just to give them time to get their trousers up."

There's certainly nothing like the odd pass to lighten the tedium of office life, nor the odd crush on your boss to make you look forward to Monday morning instead of dreading it.

You'll find too that the Personnel Lady and Judy O'Grady are nymphos under the skin. As soon as a new Adonis joins the firm, the Office Crones start dunking themselves in Devon Violets, the typing pool turn their skirts up to groin level with the office stapler, and even the senior sekketries treat themselves to a home perm and set the directors' floor throbbing with middle-aged desire.

In my experience, sex in the office is catching like the measles. Once one director discovers another director is knocking off his sekketry he starts wondering why he shouldn't have a bit on the side as well, and lust is transmitted down the hierarchy. When you consider that a boss spends more of his waking life with his sekketry than with his wife, it's hardly surprising that accidents happen.

Another contributing factor is that most women are attracted by power, and absolute power attracts absolutely. Thus the most grey, sexless men take on a lustre when they assume the mantle of Managing Director or head of the department. All women want

The most grey, sexless men

to play Egeria, but on the other hand they are seldom drawn to subordinates. I don't think Lady Chatterley's Office Boy is a viable proposition.

I think there should be lots of pretty girls in the office too. It cheers the men up if they can wolf-whistle while they work.

Some people are very clever at concealing the fact that they are having an affair with someone in the office. One woman executive I'd always thought was a pillar of respectability told me long after I'd left the firm that she'd been to bed with three members of the board in the same day: one first thing in the morning (he'd been spending the night with her), the second she took home to lunch, and the third had her for supper.

Usually, however, the couple having a walk-out congratulate themselves on being terribly discreet, carefully leaving the office at different times, meeting half-a-mile down the road and ostentatiously not speaking to each other when they meet in the passage. When in fact the forked tongues have been wagging for weeks and the whole of the building has been watching the affaire develop with passionate interest.

There are certain ways of telling

There are certain ways, too, of telling if your boss is having an affaire with someone:

If he starts getting in when the dew is still on the filing cabinets, and you're knocked sideways by the smell of *Brut for Men*.

If he keeps getting calls on the internal telephone and makes ambiguous remarks into it: "We must play this one very close to the chest, we'd better thrash the whole problem of production out over lunch. How about Overton's at 1 o'clock?"

If he comes back after a three-hour lunch ostensibly with a client, and immediately sends you out for sandwiches, or yawns his head off and spends the afternoon loudly rustling papers to disguise the fact that his stomach is rumbling.

If he and Miss Nitwit-Thompson both disappear individually but at the same time to buy the evening paper, stay away for an hour and return having forgotten to buy it.

If he and Miss Nitwit-Thompson both ring in to say they're ill with gastro-enteritis.

If he's having an affaire with someone outside the office, he'll get lots of handwritten letters marked Private and Confidential which he'll rush off to the loo to read.

DIRECT MALES
If, on the other hand, you've got designs on him yourself, your best bet will be to wait for the office party rather than the office dance, when he will be inhibited by the presence of his wife. Be careful, though. The lust that raged in his bosom on Christmas Eve can easily evaporate, and when he comes back to the office after the holiday, those burst balloons all over the floor and the fly floating in a glass of sherry on his desk may be too much for him, and he'll decide to dispense with your services altogether.

If the office wolf–who's always been a gentleman to his fingertips where you're concerned–suddenly becomes a gentleman only to his wrists and starts molesting you at every opportunity, don't slap his face (there's no point in making enemies) but tell him about your new boy friend, who's a black belt at judo and so jealous of other men he's inclined to beat them into a pulp.

If you've got your eye on one of those rising young bachelors, just say you're related to the Managing Director. You'll soon find those indecent proposals become decent ones.

If, on the other hand, you are a rising young bachelor and you want to keep the typing pool at bay, get a photograph of somebody's wife and children and put it in a leather frame on your desk.

Nor will you find it difficult to tell if one of the typists gets a crush on you. Not only will she wear her heart picked out in da-glo on her sleeve, she will also not join the general exodus at 5 p.m. but hang about waiting to be asked out for a drink. She will also make

A rising young bachelor

every possible excuse to come into your office, bringing in the morning mail one letter at a time, then coming in first with your tea, then the milk, then the sugar, then the teaspoon.

If you are an Adonis, scuffles will break out in the passage over which of the typing pool is to bring in your tea. Potted plants will bloom on your window ledge, giggling will follow you down the passage, and you will have your letters typed quicker and better than anyone else in the building.

If you want these attentions to continue, steer clear of the lot of them. Once you settle for one girl, the rest of the pool will lose interest and transfer their affections to the newly arrived Eminence Grease with the good desk-side manner.

If you fall in love with the girl, neither of you will get any work done. She will very likely take advantage of the situation and become insubordinate, lazy and forgetful. Once you get bored with her, you'll be in real trouble, for she'll be snivelling into a damp Kleenex all day and commuting back and forth to the loo. Your potted plants will wither, and the rest of the pool will mutter and glare at you. There's no divorce in the office. Death or giving in your notice is the only thing that will part you.

Finally, if you do get really keen on someone in the office, before doing anything rash like proposing marriage, get another job and see your beloved in perspective. Find out if you've got anything in common besides talking shop and evading the Office Crone, or if it was merely the fascination of the clandestine that gave an edge to the affaire.

OFFICE POLITICS

The trouble with this sinking ship is that all the rats are staying.

Apart from making and evading passes, eighty per cent of your time in any office will be spent in the area of competition: playing the power game and jockeying for position. Executives will go round after dark emptying your wastepaper basket and piecing your confidential memos together. Every time you go down the passage you'll be subjected to a party political broadcast on behalf of the Accounts Department.

Feuding goes on between person and person, and between departments, who will all try to shift blame onto each other. The Publicity Department, for example, will drive other departments into a frenzy of rage, merely because they make more noise and appear to do less work than anyone else, and consider the fact that they work late occasionally on a press party gives them the excuse to swan in late every day. The Personnel and the Accounts Departments fight with everyone. Even the Sales Department will be in a state of constant warfare with the warehouse.

Lunch at a five-star restaurant

As a young executive, sooner or later one of the directors will ask you out to lunch at a five-star restaurant. When you get to the swirling brandy stage he will start rhubarbing about getting the dead man's hand off the wheel, and then offer you a junior ministry in his Shadow Cabinet.

Don't commit yourself to joining his faction, just say you absolutely see his point. And don't let him see you going out with his rival director to another five-star lunch the next day.

Your real office Machiavelli, however, will place his own men in key positions throughout the firm and then set up:

THE PALACE REVOLUTION

A palace revolution will be heralded by the following signs:

Various top brass will start getting in unusually early in the morning, and stand about in the corridors whispering. Directors who are known to loathe each other start going out to lunch together. Strange files are suddenly sent for, urgent calls are made to the firm's accountants or solicitors from directors who normally don't deal with them. A publicity handout is run off in conditions of great secrecy and circulated to the press, who are told to treat the matter in confidence and not to release the news until they get the O.K. from the Deputy Managing Director's sekketry. The Deputy Managing Director having set the whole thing up, flies to Hamburg to see a client and waits to see what happens.

If the Managing Director is overthrown by the rest of the Board, the Deputy Managing Director will fly back and take over. If not he will deny all knowledge of the conspiracy.

The Piggies will take absolutely no notice and go to lunch.

Supplementing your income

If you work in an office there are three main ways of supplementing your income: expenses, moonlighting and getting a rise.

EXPENSES

>In Bradford, she was Mabel,
>She was Margery in Perth,
>In Plymouth, she was Phoebe,
>The sweetest girl on earth.
>In London she was Doris,
>The cutest of the bunch.
>But down on his expenses
>They were petrol, oil and lunch.

The first essential is to make friends with the cashier—
he can make things very difficult if he wants to. The
second is to hand in your expenses at least once if not
twice a week. They always seem more credible if you
present them little and often.

Cooking one's expenses is an art. In one job in which I
worked we used to set at least one day a week aside for
the purpose, and the manager, who never stirred from
the office, used to put in a regular weekly bill for £25.

And one journalist I heard of recently, who had drawn
advance expenses of over £1,500, appeared to be in
such a muddle over them that he was given a fortnight's
holiday to sort them out. Like the Evelyn Waugh
journalist who charged up £300 for camels when he
was abroad.

Expenses of course are not what they used to be. You
can't charge up £20 for fictitious lunches any more—
you have to produce bills in evidence. Ask all your
friends to save their bills for you; and you can of
course always come to some arrangement with the
local restaurateur—he gives you a sheaf of other
people's bills, and you continue to patronise his
restaurant. If the bill is outlandish, always say you
were lunching a foreigner, then it can be set against
tax.

You can also:

Travel by bus and charge up for a taxi.

Travel third class and charge up for first class.

Swim the Atlantic and charge up for the airfare.

A "round of drinks for information gained" is always
good for a fiver.

"Cloakroom and gratuities" will pull in £1 every time.

MOONLIGHTING

Moonlighting means working for two different firms
at once, and earning two salaries. This is best achieved
by slipping into one of those pockets of inefficiency in

a big firm where you've plenty of spare time on your hands.

I've moonlighted most of my working career. It began when I joined a large firm of publishers and, realising there wasn't enough work for me, I got another job as a fiction editor on a magazine. It was a full-time job, but then I had a typewriter, a sekketry, a telephone and a post-room to handle all the mail.

I used to reach the office at 8.30 every morning, and rattle away at my fiction editing. Everyone in the publishing firm thought I was working like a slave – so they left me alone. I used to claim expenses from both jobs, and my cup was full when I got rises from both companies at Christmas.

Occasionally there were complications when both jobs got busy simultaneously, and telephone calls came through on the publisher's switchboard asking for me as the fiction editor. I used to feel a bit like a man with a wife and a mistress who were both complaining he wasn't paying them enough attention.

My favourite moonlighter was a girl who joined one of my previous firms as a sekketry. Peculiar men kept ringing her up, and she was always slipping out of the office for four-hour lunches. Eventually after six months we discovered she was working as a prostitute on the side.

Another way you can supplement your income is to ask for a rise.

HOW TO GET A RISE OUT OF SOMEONE

Go to your boss and say you've been offered a fabulous job, you don't want to take it but with a wife and six parrots to support you've simply got to think of their interests first. If you're any good they'll give you a rise to keep you.

Beware, though. I heard the other day of a man who

tried precisely this tactic:

Him: I've been offered this fabulous job etc.

Boss: Good for you. You had better take it then, hadn't you? When do you start?

Exit friend jobless and speechless.

You can also borrow so much money from the firm on a paying-back basis that they've got to give you a rise ever to get their money back.

Borrow a pregnant lady

Or invite your pregnant wife or borrow a pregnant lady and parade her up and down as often as you can in the office in gym shoes with holes in, and keep a photograph of seven children on your desk (you can always get such photographs from agencies).

The logical way of course is to work harder, but make

sure everyone realises it.

In one firm, one of the junior sekketries typed the following letter to the Managing Director:

"Dear Sir,

I would like to thank you for my rise of £1. I will do my bust to justify your faith in me."

HOW NOT TO GIVE SOMEONE A RISE

Miss Nitwit-Thompson asks for a rise.

Send for her, get out a file which says *Nitwit-Thompson, Confidential* and leave it in a prominent position on your desk. Don't look up for five minutes when she comes into your office. Then ask her to sit down, and flip meditatively through her confidential file, frowning a great deal.

Look up and say: "We're very overloaded with deadwood in this firm, you know." (Long pause to make her jumpy.) "We've got to hack it out before we can give anyone a rise."

Then get out a very complicated chart with everyone's salary on it, look at it for a few minutes, then say: "You're getting a great deal more than anyone else your age. I wonder how that came about?" (Another long pause.)

And Miss Nitwit-Thompson slinks out of your office terrified you're going to dock her wages.

Other ways you can avoid giving someone a rise include:

Praising their work inordinately and promoting them to something meaningless like: Special Director or Deputy Assistant to the Personnel Manager.

Giving them more responsibility.

Offering to have their offices painted for them.

Upgrading their company car from an 1100 to an 1800 – in the figures lies the deceit. They can then say they've got a rise of 700 and forget to mention the cc's.

The firing squad

The management of a large agency decided overnight to axe 80 per cent of their creative staff and hired a hatchet man to fire them in triplicate. After he'd finished his dirty work, they fired him as well.

If a boss is unsatisfied with the work of a member of his staff, he should send for him, find out whether his inefficiency is due to family trouble, sickness etc. and if not, give him a rocket and warn him that unless he improves radically he will be given a month's notice at the end of the month. Too many bosses sack their staff without giving them a chance to do better, or without them realising their work is unsatisfactory.

Even more insidious is the freezing out method practised by managements who will do anything to avoid a direct confrontation.

The procedure is as follows:

Stage One: You are suddenly no longer asked to meetings or 'cc'ed on memos, your name is removed from the magazine circulation list, people stop talking as you walk down the passage. Your sekketry starts forgetting to water your plants and spends her time taking letters from the newly arrived whizz-kid/ certified rat, who's currently working in the passage outside your office.

Stage Two: As your paranoia intensifies, you are given less and less to do and office juniors start cheeking you, until . . .

Stage Three: You arrive on Monday morning to find the whizz kid installed in your office, his name beside yours on the door. During the week his furniture is moved in until you're both perching on top of the filing cabinet.

Stage Four: You turn up the following Monday to find your desk in the passage, so, self-respect in tatters, you finally get the message and start looking for another job.

If you're under contract it's more tricky for them to boot you out, but they get round it by transferring you to outer Alaska at a vastly reduced salary and refusing to pay your wife and parrot's fare.

Another ruse is to wait until you go on holiday. You stagger in from the beach too blinded at first by the sun to read the registered letter bidding you take your disservices somewhere else.

Turn the tables

Of course there are numerous things you can do to turn the tables on the people who've sacked you – like Napoleon's Finance Minister, who crippled the country's entire monetary system by retiring into his office for three days and burning every document he could lay his hands on. Or the man in the sweet factory who wrote four-letter words instead of "Welcome to Blackpool" in the inside of half a mile of rock.

Some people avenge themselves by spending their last month appropriating office property: writing paper, sugar, paper clips, elastic bands. A man I know completely equipped his new flat with office furniture. One evening when he was struggling out of the building with a bookcase he met the chairman, who did not realise it was company property and gave him a helping hand to the car.

N.B. Sometimes—even if you know you're for the chop—it's a good idea to hang on. In one firm, two directors came to the conclusion that one of their executives was useless and decided to fire him. Both of them assumed the other one would do it, and nothing happened for eighteen months, by which time they decided he could stay on as he'd got more experience.

Social occasions

THE OFFICE OUTING

Whether it's *Tulip Time in Spalding, Lincs.*, *A Charity Walk to Gravesend* or *A Night out in London's Theatreland*, this beastly romp is loathed both by the people who go on it, and by the people who organise it. It's a hangover from feudal forelock-tugging times, when the Lords of the Manor used to give charity banquets for the poor. It should be abolished and the money spent on extra bonuses.

THE LEAVING PARTY

In some offices, there's a permanent round of parties after work. Either you're celebrating landing a big contract, or cheering each other up for losing it, or saying good-bye to someone, or wishing them happy birthday, or celebrating the fact that their cat's just had kittens.

Leaving parties are occasions when sex rears its ugly head, for while you are saying good-bye to dear old Fothers from Production who's been with the firm for forty years, you will probably drink enough to say a big hello to Miss Twink from the typing pool, whose knickers are bursting into flames at the thought of you.

Hardly a day passes either without some office junior coming round waving a manilla envelope collecting for someone's birthday or leaving present – executives will be considered very mean if they give less than 50p, and directors must give at least £1. Later in the day you will have to add your name at an acute angle to a myriad others on a leaving card. It is interesting to note how much more talent and imagination manifests itself in leaving cards than in any other project produced by the art or copy departments; it is the one example of work that is not fettered by red tape or mucked about by senior members of the hierarchy.

THE OFFICE DANCE

Another beastly romp. Attendance is usually "optional", but it's frowned upon if you don't turn up. All the warehouse comes up for the evening, their wives with sequinned hair and fat shoulders bulging over strapless satin. The office slut who's been slopping around all year in bedroom slippers, her dyed orange hair going black at the roots, immediately turns into a swan and hooks half the men in the room.

You are expected to sit down to a five-course dinner at five o'clock in the evening when no one's at all hungry except the Piggies.

The seating plan is devised by some sadist in the

basement who sees that you are not placed next to anyone you know, so you exchange platitudes with some Latvian packer's wife, as you plough valiantly through lumps of sole and bombes surprises, then have to listen to inaudible speeches.

Afterwards the high and mighty unbend enough to dance and there are Paul Joneses which turn into a rugger scrum because all the typing pool are fighting tooth and nail to end up opposite the office Adonis.

Always dance with the boss's wife—she is officially your hostess.

Always dance with the senior sekketries and your own sekketry.

Be careful not to beat the directors at musical chairs— one man who did, sank without trace in the New Year. Let them win all the spot prizes.

Bar propping is, alas, much disapproved of.

Look cheerful, stay vertical. The opportunists will be out in force giving the impression they are having the night of their lives, and being seen by the Managing Director to be good mixers.

The only interest lies in seeing members of the staff's wives and husbands for the first time. Who would have thought mildewed Mr Meed from Packaging would turn up with such a corker? And Mrs Higgins from Production has always left early on the grounds that her husband beats her up if she's not home by six to give him his tea. He turns out to be half her size with thinning hair and a stutter.

THE CHRISTMAS PARTY

Finally there's the Office Christmas Party—subtly different from the Office Dance, because no wives or husbands or lovers are invited to inhibit the fun.

This is a typical office party:

It's Christmas Eve in the workhouse. The typing pool has been transformed into a fairy grotto. The typists are red-faced from the hairdresser's and blowing up balloons—they have been making furtive trips to the Ladies all afternoon to see if their dresses have hung out properly. Excitement seethes. This is the night when supertax husbands are hooked. In other parts of the building the higher echelons anticipate the evening with trepidation and veiled lust. The building already reverberates with revelry. The Art Department, having declared U.D.I., held their party before midday and are still going strong.

At 4.55, when it's too late to rush out and get her something, the Office Crone makes everyone feel a louse by handing out gaily wrapped presents. At 5.00 everyone stops typing in mid-word and thunders down to the Ladies which soon resembles the changing room at The Way In. The office junior has used hair lacquer under her arms instead of deodorant and is walking round like a penguin.

The party begins with everyone standing under the fluorescent lighting wondering what to say next—strange, considering they find no difficulty during working hours. Miss Nitwit-Thompson, who has been putting her Christmas cards through the franking machine all afternoon and telephoning her friends to say what a bore the party is going to be, has not bothered to change out of her grey jersey dress. She will be leaving after five minutes to catch a train home to Daddy.

In an attempt to please everyone, the £80 collected for drink has been spent on one bottle of everything from Brown Ale to Babycham. The caretaker who is manning the bar has assembled a strange collection of glasses: flower vases, toothmugs, bakelite cups. The Office Wolf is busy lacing the typists' orange juice with vodka.

Neatly displayed in out-trays is food cooked by members of the staff; curling sandwiches, flaccid

cheese straws with baker's droop, and an aggressive-
looking Christmas cake covered in festive robins
baked by the Office Crone. The Piggies have already
got their heads down in the trough.

Conversation is still laboured, but the arrival of the
Production department, who've been boozing all day
on free liquor, helps to jolly things along. Soon,
members of the Board drift down from Olympus,
genial from a succession of long Christmas lunches.

The Receptionist, who is not famed for the strength
of her knicker elastic, is making a very alive set at
the handsome director of Public Relations. Miss
Nitwit-Thompson discovers she's met the Managing
Director's son at a number of dinner parties. Soon
they are nose to nose.

People are relaxing. Someone puts on a record and
two typists dance together. One of the young men on
the make is overheard boasting about his expenses
by the Financial Director and loses his chance of
promotion. The office cat has wriggled out of his green
Xmas bow and is thoughtfully licking fish paste out of
the sandwiches.

Faces are reddening, backs are being slapped, people
are passing round packets of fifty cigarettes. The
Managing Director needs little encouragement to
get up and say what a big happy family they all are.

The Office Junior swells with pride at the thought that
she and about 400 other people are entirely responsible
for the firm's turnover. The caretaker takes the
opportunity to rinse some glasses in the fire bucket.

A packer arrives from the warehouse with shiny blue
suit and horny hands, and claims a dance with one of
the senior sekketries, who bends over backwards to
avoid his four-ale breath. The Receptionist and the
Director of Public Relations are having private
relations behind the filing cabinet.

The Managing Director's wife, who has come to

Claims a dance with a senior sekketry

collect her husband, has taken a piece of Christmas
cake in deference to the typing pool. She didn't realise
the robins were made of plaster, and is now desperately
trying to spit out a beak.

Lust is rising in the vast jacked-up bosom of Miss
Hitler from Personnel, and she is jostling the newest
trainee towards the mistletoe. The Office Boy has
hiccups and is trying to roll cheese and chutney
sandwiches into an electric typewriter.

"God bless you all, Merry Christmas," cries the
departing Managing Director.

Now he's gone the fun is unconfined. There is a general
unfastening of chastity belts. The Sales Director is
playing bears round the furniture, the Office Wolf

Lust is rising

keeps turning off the lights. Squeaks and scuffles break
out in nearby offices. The oldest member of the staff is
telling anyone who will listen how the firm grew from
a tiny two-room business to the "great concern we
are today". The Director of Public Relations is in
the Gents desperately scrubbing lipstick from his
shirt front.

The drink has run out. Miss Nitwit-Thompson, who
is now quite giggly, is being taken to Annabels by the
Managing Director's son. She'll be lucky if she gets
home to Daddy before Boxing Day.

Reluctant to end the evening, people are making plans

to meet in pubs or the backs of cars. Others are saying "Merry Christmas", exchanging beery kisses and taking uncertain steps towards the nearest bus stop.

The caretaker, who has appropriated several bottles of drink, shakes his head over the pair of rose-pink pants in the Gents. Under a pile of forgotten coats and umbrellas lies a doll's tea set and a mournful-looking turkey. As he locks up, a telephone rings unaccountably in one of the lifts.